Do Bhrian Fear Cróga

Someone Who'll Watch Over Me was first performed at the Hampstead Theatre, on 10 July 1992. The cast was as follows:

MICHAEL	Alec McCowen
ADAM	Hugh Quarshie
EDWARD	Stephen Rea
Director	Robin Lefèvre
Designer	Robin Don
Lighting Designer	Nick Chelton

Artistic Director for the Hampstead Theatre: Jenny Topper

SETTING: A cell
TIME: Now

PROLOGUE

In Darkness ADAM's *voice is heard humming lowly, 'Someone to Watch Over Me'. His voice grows slightly louder as light slowly rises. He stops singing. The light now just about picks out his shape.*

SCENE ONE

Complete light. Ella Fitzgerald sings 'Someone to Watch Over Me'. EDWARD *and* ADAM *are together in the cell. They are separately chained to the walls.* EDWARD *is centre stage;* ADAM *is stage right. The chains are of sufficient length to allow freedom of movement for both men to exercise.*
EDWARD *is dressed in a loose blue T-shirt and white football shorts.* ADAM *is dressed in black T-shirt and grey shorts.*
They exercise in silence. ADAM's *exercises are rigorous;* EDWARD *moves through his paces more sluggishly.*

EDWARD: That was Ella Fitzgerald singing, 'Someone To Watch Over Me'.
ADAM: What was?
EDWARD: My eighth and final record for *Desert Island Discs*. It is also my single choice of record. Good old Ella. Did you have *Desert Island Discs* in America?
ADAM: No. What is it?
EDWARD: You pick eight records and your favourite among the eight. Then you choose a luxury. Then a book, apart from the Bible and Shakespeare. They're already on the desert island. My book is a guide to home-brewing beer, and my luxury is a beer-making kit. And Ella Fitzgerald would sing to me. I'd be happy on a desert island. Easy pleased, that's me. An easy-going man.
(*Silence.*)
Jesus, the boredom, the boredom, the bloody boredom. And they're coming up the hill at Cheltenham and Dawn Run is

I

fading, she is fading, the great Irish mare will not complete
the unique double of the Cheltenham Hurdle and the Gold
Cup, she's tiring and she jumps the fence, she's gaining
strength in the air, she's wearing them down, she passes one,
she passes two, a third she passes and the winning post's in
sight, she's done it, she's won. Dawn Run for Ireland,
mighty woman. She's won the Gold Cup.
(*Silence.*)
Jesus, it was a real pity I didn't have money riding on her.
Dawn Run. Did I ever tell you about Dawn Run?
ADAM: She was your favourite horse. She won both her great
races. She was magnificent. You loved her and would have
married her, but it couldn't have worked out. She was a
horse and you were human. Besides, she was Protestant, you
were Catholic, and you were already married. You've told
me about Dawn Run.
EDWARD: Sarcastic yankee. She was a hero, that horse.
ADAM: So were Glasgow Celtic when they won the European Cup,
and I don't want to hear about them, either.
(*Silence.* ADAM *exercises strenuously.*)
How many press-ups did you do?
EDWARD: Didn't count.
ADAM: How many?
EDWARD: Twenty.
ADAM: You did not.
EDWARD: Fifteen.
ADAM: You did not.
EDWARD: Twelve.
ADAM: Eleven. One more than yesterday.
EDWARD: Yes.
ADAM: Come on, Edward, we've got to keep going. I got to get
you into condition. You know that, you agreed to it. We can
have competitions when you're in condition.
EDWARD: I don't care about competitions or about my condition.
(*Silence.*)
ADAM: Yea, yea, I know what you mean. Who am I fooling? Who
the hell am I fooling? Me. That's who. No, no brooding. No
blaming myself. That way I go under. I will not go under.

(*Silence.*)

EDWARD: The boredom, the boredom, Jesus, the boredom.

(*Silence.*)

I'm going to start to brood.

ADAM: I will not brood.

EDWARD:I'm going to start to blame myself.

ADAM: Don't.

EDWARD: I'm imagining where I would be, if I hadn't come to this country.

ADAM: Where would you be if you hadn't come here?

EDWARD: At home wondering what it would be like to be here.

ADAM:Yea.

(EDWARD *laughs.*)

EDWARD: There's some that cannot stay at home, and our Eddie, he is one of them. My father's words, proved right, proved right. Time and time again. He has to be the big man, this boy, never getting stale, never being safe. And look where he's landed today. Far across the sea. Not in Amerikay nor even in Australia, but in the land of the fucking Lebanon. Jesus, could I have found it on the map before I came here? I leave one kip at home to come to this kip here – oh Christ, look at this place. The dirt of it. Chained to a wall. No women. Food's fit for pigs. You don't know if it's morning or night. You don't know who belonging to you is alive or dead. You can't even go to the shithouse without one of them handcuffed to you, watching your very bowels move. The heat, the dust, the smell. It's a bad hole. But I will say one thing. It's better than being in Strabane.

ADAM: What's wrong with Strabane?

EDWARD: If you ever want proof there's no God, go to Strabane. Hell on a stick, sweet Strabane. It's not as bad as Omagh. Omagh, Omagh, God protect us all from Omagh. Omagh has a cathedral and a hospital in it. The hospital is slightly more reminiscent of Chartres. I screwed this woman in Omagh one night. When I looked at her in the sober light of morning, I thought she was a man.

ADAM: Were you married at the time you screwed with her?

EDWARD: Don't remember. Why do you ask?

3

ADAM: Making conversation.

EDWARD: You're making judgements.

ADAM: I don't make judgements.

EDWARD: No, you just listen. Let me ramble on, you store it all up, then you size it up. Well, after two months sizing it up, what kind of specimen do you make of me? What kind of childhood would you say I had?

ADAM: Remarkably happy, I'd guess. You don't mention your mother. That's unusual. Something else is unusual. You barely talk about your own kids.

EDWARD: Barely.

ADAM: Why?

(*Silence.*)

After two months, can't you tell me?

EDWARD: I don't know them. Working too hard, playing too hard, me. Like father, like son in that respect. I didn't know him until it was too late. I don't know them. Now I never will. Because we're going to be in here for a long time. They could be grown men and women by the time I next see them. If I next see them.

ADAM: You're an Irishman. You're from a neutral country. They'll let you go.

EDWARD: Didn't I think that? Wasn't it me waving the green passport in their faces, roaring, 'Ireland, Ireland'? They still stuck the gun up my arse and dragged me in here. Green passport, neutral country? What's that to these boys? Save your breath, Adam. We'll be old men before we're out of here. We're stuck here.

(*Silence.*)

We're stuck here.

(ADAM *begins to exercise again.*)

For the love of God, will you give it a rest? Do yous Americans ever stand still?

ADAM: Would you prefer I were an Arab?

EDWARD: I don't go for Arabs that much. The sand blows up their skirts and they're not allowed to scratch themselves. The itch has them the way they are, excitable.

ADAM: You're pretty excitable yourself today.

4

EDWARD: And you never are?

ADAM: I don't take it out on you if I am.

EDWARD: You should. It might give me something to fight against.

ADAM: I dislike fighting.

EDWARD: Do you really dislike it? I thought the fighting was our business, in our own ways. I report it, you – what do you do about the fighting? When we were covering the Northern bother, the boys we really hated were the Italians. I remember why. Their big interest was in photographing kids. Kids crying, kids cut to pieces, preferably dead kids.

ADAM: I am not interested in dead kids. I am not a photographer.

EDWARD: No, you're – what? Someone that makes the fighting all nice and clean and scientific. You stand back and examine the effects of war on innocent young minds. How very kind, doctor. Disturbed young minds. You want them disturbed, don't you, doctor? Research, publish, profit, as I said. Make your money. Like myself, Adam. Doing a job. Very professional, Adam. Very profitable. Very American.

ADAM: You piece of shit.

EDWARD: Money, Adam, you were in it for the money.

ADAM: And what the hell were you in it for? By your own dirty admission –

EDWARD: It was my dirty admission. I say I came here for the money. You don't, but you did. So, who's the piece of shit? You are.

ADAM: I want to crack your fucking face open. I'm going to fucking kill you. If I've to listen to you much longer, I will kill you.

EDWARD: You can't, Adam. Even if you could, you haven't got that in you.

ADAM: Shut up.

EDWARD: You're not a killer. Isn't that a good thing, doctor?

ADAM: They haven't broken me yet.

EDWARD: The Arabs? No, but I've broken you, Adam. Haven't I?

ADAM: Nearly. Why?

EDWARD: About time, I've broken you. You think you've all the answers. You don't. I got through to something in you that you don't have an answer for. Whatever that cool head is hiding, I do not know, but I do know that cool's going to

5

crack, it has to, and we'd better both be prepared for when it does. Whatever else about this place, we're in it together, we have to stick it out together. We'll come out of this alive. One favour – let me be able to do my worst to you, and you be able to do your worst to me. Is that agreed? That way, as you say, they won't break us, for we'll be too used to fighting for our lives.

ADAM: Will we get out alive?

(*Silence.*)

I do get scared. I miss my home.

EDWARD: That's all I wanted to hear you say.

ADAM: I've said it. All right?

EDWARD: One step nearer home, saying it.

ADAM: Ed, don't break me. Don't let me go mad. Say you want to go home as well.

(*Silence.*)

EDWARD: I want to go home.

ADAM: Say it again.

EDWARD: I want to go home.

ADAM: It's all right, Edward.

EDWARD: I want my wife.

ADAM: She's all right.

EDWARD: My kids, I want to see them.

ADAM: You will.

EDWARD: My wife, my kids, please, let me see them. God, please. Let me talk to them. Let me go home.

ADAM: No.

EDWARD:, I want to go home. Arabs, Arabs –

ADAM: No.

(*Silence.*)

EDWARD: We're going mad.

ADAM: We're in Lebanon.

EDWARD: Yes.

ADAM: I'm in Lebanon.

EDWARD: So am I.

(EDWARD *sings 'Someone to Watch Over Me'. His voice fades as the music of the song plays. Lights fade.*)

The music of the song continues to play as the light rises.
MICHAEL *has joined them in the cell. He too is bare-footed,*
wearing a white T-shirt and black shorts. He is chained to the wall,
stage left.
MICHAEL *sleeps.* ADAM *reads the Bible, the Koran sits open beside*
it. EDWARD *lies slumped, watching* MICHAEL.

EDWARD: Still no sign of life out of the new boy. How long do you
    think he'll be conked out for?
ADAM: He should be awake soon.
EDWARD: Poor bollocks. He's in for a bit of a shock if he expects
    daylight. He must be out cold for the best part of twelve
    hours. Yea, I'd say he'd soon come to.
ADAM: Yea, he should.
EDWARD: A bit of new company would liven the place up. I hope
    he speaks English. Jesus, I hope this isn't the start of a rush
    hour as well. How many of us do you think they could stick
    in the one room?
ADAM: I don't know, Edward.
EDWARD: At least they've left him his bottle of water. If he
    wakens with a thirst on him he can drown it. Drown your
    sorrows, boy, dry your tears. Mourning and weeping in this
    valley of tears.
ADAM: Biblical.
EDWARD: What?
ADAM: Valley of tears.
EDWARD: Is that what you're reading? The Bible?
ADAM: Yea.
EDWARD: It's nice of them to leave us the Bible and the Koran.
ADAM: They pass the time.
EDWARD: For you.
ADAM: If you want to read either they're here for you.
EDWARD: Not a chance. I hate religion. All religion. Bad for you.
ADAM: It passes the time.
EDWARD: Religion?
ADAM: Reading.

7

EDWARD: Why are the Irish so religious?
ADAM: Why?
EDWARD: I've asked the question.
ADAM: I suppose because they're always thanking God.
EDWARD: What for?
ADAM: That they're not Belgian.
EDWARD: I think your man looks a bit Belgian. Maybe he's
   German. I hope he's not.
   (*Silence.*)
   The Germans and the Dutch, they're buying up the whole
   West of Ireland. 'No Trespassing' notices everywhere.
   (*Silence.*)
   It would be rough for him if he couldn't speak English.
ADAM: I speak German. A little German.
EDWARD: Good for you.
ADAM: You find it objectionable that I speak German?
EDWARD: A little, shitehead.
ADAM: I am not a shithead.
EDWARD: I said 'shitehead', not 'shithead', shitehead.
   (*Silence.* ADAM *returns to reading.*)
   Great expression that. 'Shitehead.' I like it.
   (*Silence.*)
   You should quit reading in this light. It'll blind your eyes.
   (*Silence.*)
   It's funny, you rarely see an Arab wearing glasses.
ADAM: They don't masturbate.
EDWARD: How do they manage?
ADAM: Do you? Masturbate?
EDWARD: Never.
ADAM: Nor me.
EDWARD: Well, not before six o'clock in the morning. You have
   to have some morality.
ADAM: My record is fifteen times in one night, and I made no
   complaints against myself.
EDWARD: Any Arab women?
ADAM: Just American girls. I like American girls.
EDWARD: I had a fantasy about an Arab woman. She was only
   wearing a yashmak. I was wearing a grass skirt.

8

ADAM: Why?

EDWARD: She was kinky. I like that. It makes a woman unique. It was a good fantasy.

ADAM: I like a little foreplay in mine.

EDWARD: Foreplay? In a fantasy.

ADAM: Don't the Irish like foreplay?

EDWARD: We invented foreplay. We call it drink.

ADAM: What turns your wife on?

EDWARD: A bottle of vodka. What about your woman?

ADAM: She's Californian. She likes to imagine she's sleeping with God. This would turn her on. The Song of Songs, which is Solomon's. 'Let him kiss me with the kisses of his mouth, for thy love is better than wine . . . Whither is my beloved turned aside? My beloved's I am, and my beloved is mine . . . Make haste, my beloved, and be thou like to a roe or to a young hart upon the mountain of spices.'

EDWARD: Not bad. I could see some women going for that.

ADAM: I could turn her on, then she can turn me on.

EDWARD: How?

ADAM: She tells me I've a dick that could choke a donkey.

EDWARD: Jesus, some dick.

ADAM: Some donkey.

MICHAEL: I'm terribly sorry, but where am I?

EDWARD: So it's yourself, is it?

MICHAE: Pardon?

EDWARD: Do you not recognize me? We were at school together.

MICHAEL: I don't think so.

EDWARD: Eton, wasn't it? Or Harrow?

MICHAEL: No, I don't – where am I?

EDWARD: In the officer's mess, Brit Boy. A bit rough and ready, but you'll get used to it. We have. So, how's the outside world?

MICHAEL: Who are you? Why am I here?

EDWARD: To see a movie. Maybe if you're lucky there'll be a meal afterwards.

ADAM: Let it rest, Edward. Are you OK, fella?

(MICHAEL *is half hysterical*.)

MICHAEL: I simply wish to know where I am and who you are.

EDWARD: Lower your voice, bollocks, you want us to get a hiding?

MICHAEL: I was on my way to the market and I was looking for fruit, for pears, for I had invited a few people from the university for dinner and for dessert I wanted to make a pear flan, I was walking to the market –

EDWARD: A pear flan?

MICHAEL: For dessert. I have people invited for dinner.

EDWARD: Then they're going to go hungry, sweetheart.

MICHAEL: Why am I chained to a wall?

ADAM: You've been taken hostage!

MICHAEL: Kidnapped?

EDWARD: Yes.

ADAM: My name's Adam Canning. I'm an American.

EDWARD: Edward Sheridan. Irish.

MICHAEL: I'm an Englishman.

EDWARD: Of course you are.

MICHAEL: Who has kidnapped me?

ADAM: We don't know for sure.

EDWARD: They're not terribly chatty.

MICHAEL: Why have they kidnapped me?

EDWARD: Because you're an Englishman. How dreadfully unfair. Not cricket.

MICHAEL: Why have they taken away all my clothes?

ADAM: They want to make double sure you stay.

MICHAEL: Oh my God, I am chained to a wall.

EDWARD: So you are. So are fucking we. So you better enjoy it.

MICHAEL: What do you mean, 'enjoy it'?

EDWARD: It's a laugh, isn't it, Adam? That's how we get by. Laughing at it all. Do you not enjoy a laugh? Have you no sense of humour?

ADAM: Stop freezing the guy out.

MICHAEL: How long have you been here?

ADAM: Four months.

EDWARD: Two months.

MICHAEL: My name is Michael. Michael Watters.

EDWARD: So what's up in the outside world, Mick? Do you mind me calling you Mick? Is there much word about us?

MICHAEL: I'm sorry?

EDWARD: Do people talk about us? Have you heard anything about our people? What are they doing to release us?

MICHAEL: I don't know.

EDWARD: What do you mean, you don't know?

MICHAEL: I had barely arrived in Beirut, I really wasn't well acquainted with anyone –

EDWARD: People must have been talking about us –

MICHAEL: People would mention in passing –

EDWARD: 'Mention in passing'? Do they know what we're going through?

ADAM: Are we forgotten?

MICHAEL: They get on with their lives. If they thought too much about it, about you, they'd – they'd –

ADAM: What?

(*Silence.*)

They'd what?

MICHAEL: I don't know. I really don't know anything about the political situation in Lebanon. I came here to teach English. I lecture in English. That's all. That's why I was asking people round to dinner. To learn the ropes a little. I was going to the market. I wanted to buy pears for dessert. They stopped me. They had guns. I was so frightened. I told them I was simply a teacher of English at the university. I was so frightened. God, where am I? Please, let me go. Let me go.

ADAM: That's enough. You mustn't let them hear you cry. They're listening to you as you speak. They want you to weep. Don't ever do that in here. I'm warning you, don't weep. That's what they want. So don't cry. Laugh. Do you hear me? Laugh.

MICHAEL: I can't.

ADAM: Laugh, damn you.

MICHAEL: No.

(EDWARD *starts to laugh loudly. He stops.* ADAM *laughs loudly,* EDWARD *joining in. They stop.*)

ADAM: Go, Michael. Laugh.

(*Silence.*)

Laugh.

(MICHAEL *laughs.*)
More.
(MICHAEL *laughs more loudly.* ADAM *and* EDWARD *join in his laughter. They stop.* ADAM *signals* MICHAEL *to continue laughing. He does so.*)
Good guy. That's what you got to do. They've heard you laughing.
MICHAEL: What will they do now?
ADAM: Wait and see.
(*Silence.*)
They're in a peaceful mood tonight.
EDWARD: They're not even laughing back.
ADAM: Mission accomplished, Michael. Stage one.
MICHAEL: Who are they?
EDWARD: The enemy.
ADAM: The food's OK. We are given a bottle of water each day. They let us use the bathroom, but they go with us. We are never alone. We've managed so far. We are always in these chains, that is so degrading. We are given the Bible and the Koran to read. But the worst of all is that we have no way of knowing what is going on in the outside world.
EDWARD: We can't even listen to the BBC World Service.
ADAM: No, we can't.
EDWARD: No contact with the outside world; that goes about its business.
ADAM: That's the way it is in Chinatown.
(*Silence.*)
EDWARD: Are you a married man?
MICHAEL: Widowed, I'm afraid, some years ago. No children.
EDWARD: Any dogs?
MICHAEL: A cocker spaniel and a golden retriever. They're at my mother's home. Near Peterborough. She lives –
(*Silence.*)
She lives there. Near Peterborough.
(*Silence.*)
ADAM: I was a doctor.
EDWARD: You still are. Journalist, me.
MICHAEL: I lost my university post. They're not teaching much

Old and Middle English these days. A dying concern.
Rationalization of resources. They say. So when I could only
get employment here, I came here. I absolutely need to
work. I was warned about the danger. I was worried. But I
refused to be afraid. So I came here.
ADAM: And got caught.
MICHAEL: Yes.
EDWARD: Yes.
　(*Silence*.)
　Are you all right?
ADAM: You'll get used to it. In time.
　(*Silence*.)
EDWARD: Who was coming to dinner?
MICHAEL: I'm making a pear flan.
　(*Silence*.)
　I thought everything was going very well, very well indeed,
　but just when I'm about to pop it into the oven, gas mark 7, I
　discover I can't find the pears. The pears. I'd forgotten the
　pears.
　(*Lights fade*.)

SCENE THREE

EDWARD *browses through the Koran.* MICHAEL *sits with his eyes
closed.* ADAM *is running on the spot.*

ADAM: I wish we could go to see a movie.
EDWARD: Uum.
ADAM: Jeez, I'd enjoy a good movie.
MICHAEL: Yes.
EDWARD: Do you like pictures?
MICHAEL: I do.
EDWARD: You might have struck me more as a book man.
　(*Silence*.)
MICHAEL: I do enjoy a good book as well.
　(*Silence*.)
　I would prefer at the moment to see a movie.

EDWARD: Why are you calling them movies? Do the English not
  call them films?
MICHAEL: I just called it a movie. Why do you object?
EDWARD: It just sounded strange.
MICHAEL: Oh, sorry.
EDWARD: Why are you sorry?
MICHAEL: That I didn't call it a film, if it offended you.
EDWARD: It didn't.
MICHAEL: Then why did you bring it up?
EDWARD: Something to say.
  (ADAM *stops running*.)
ADAM: I wish we could go to see a movie.
EDWARD: You've said that. We've heard you.
ADAM: Yea.
  (*Silence*.)
MICHAEL: I don't think I'd like to be a film star.
EDWARD: Why not?
MICHAEL: I imagine being an actor is quite a boring life.
EDWARD: Yea.
ADAM: Yea.
  (*Silence*.)
EDWARD: Aye, boring.
ADAM: Yea.
MICHAEL: Yes.
EDWARD: No.
MICHAEL: No.
EDWARD: What do you mean, 'no'? You've just said yes.
MICHAEL: I was agreeing with you. I thought you were agreeing
  with me. So I said no.
EDWARD: You say no when you're agreeing with someone?
MICHAEL: If they've said no, yes.
EDWARD: Yes or no, what is it?
MICHAEL: What?
EDWARD: Shut up.
  (*Silence*.)
  Let's see a movie. Shoot the movie. An Englishman comes to
  Lebanon.
ADAM: Being well trained in the social graces, he invites people to

14

dinner. He does not necessarily like these people, but they speak English, and they would seem to know the ropes about this place, so they may help him to endure his time here. He will feed them. There is only one problem. Food. He will take his courage in both hands and walk through the city of Beirut looking for food to cook. To his surprise he sees at some distance from him the very same people he has invited to dinner. He calls to them, but they don't answer. He calls again, he follows them, and they are going into districts of Beirut he does not know. He follows them, he finds himself trapped, he sees them ahead of him, still he calls out. They look back. They leave him. The film ends. (*Silence.*)
Hitchcock. That's who made that movie.
EDWARD: I can't stick Hitchcock.
ADAM: Why?
EDWARD: His endings.
ADAM: Yca.
(*Silence.*)
Shoot another movie.
EDWARD: A nun comes to Beirut. She has come to do her Christian duty to the orphans of that troubled city. She first befriends a goat wandering through this war-torn town. She greets the goat as a long-lost ally, singing to it on her guitar. Little children hear her song and join in, miraculously learning English. Our happy band join forces, they fight the cruel foe, they convert the whole of Lebanon to the great task in hand – love thy neighbour. Not everyone is pleased with Sister's success. She is shot, as is her guitar. One of the little children presses the bullet-strewn instrument to her body as they carry away the corpse of the dead nun.
ADAM: Played by Madonna.
EDWARD: As they carry off the corpse, vultures gather. They eye the dead nun hungrily.
ADAM: They swoop in their throng down on the dead body. They start to tear her flesh. A band of machismo Arabs arrive on white steeds. The horses' flesh contrasts in their beauty with the shattered flesh of the dead virgin. They

draw their guns. The shoot off the vultures' heads.

EDWARD: Sam Peckinpah Productions.

MICHAEL: In the midst of this horror music is heard. A man preaching peace moves through this machismo crowd. He is dressed in a loincloth. He speaks against violence. He speaks of civilization. He is a man of peace.

ADAM: Richard Fucking Attenborough movie.

EDWARD: Fortunately at that moment a crowd of peasants dance on to the scene, waving scythes. Immaculately photographed, they win the hearts of the cruel Arabs, for among the peasants there is one disabled who has a dream – to be an artist. With the help of his mother, and his own determination, he finally wins an Oscar, which he collects with his ear –

ADAM: Oh Jesus, not an Irish movie, please –

EDWARD: And they live happily ever after.

(*Silence.*)

We're fucked.

MICHAEL: So it seems.

EDWARD: How are you feeling?

(*Silence.*)

Come on, give us a dose of the stiff upper lip. Raise our morale, old boy. Tell us all about the war. So many chappies went through what we're going through. Fine example to us all. Let's hear it for the British!

(*Silence.*)

You're a miserable git, Aren't you? There's not much life in you. Is there?

(*Silence.*)

MICHAEL: I'm no more afraid of you than I am of them.

EDWARD: Stiff upper lip, let's hear it for –

MICHAEL: I mean it. I'm not afraid of you.

ADAM: He's not afraid of you, Edward.

EDWARD: He's not afraid of you, Adam.

ADAM: He's not afraid of anything.

EDWARD: No, he's not.

MICHAEL: In this dreadful situation –

EDWARD: In this dreadful situation –

MICHAEL: Where we have found ourselves –
EDWARD: Where we have found ourselves –
MICHAEL: I fail to see how tormenting me –
EDWARD: I fail to see –
MICHAEL: Will in any way alleviate –
EDWARD: Alleviate – alleviate – alleviate – alleviate – alleviate.
MICHAEL: Do you wish me to admit I'm afraid of you?
(*Silence.*)
Is that what you wish me to do?
(*Silence.*)
Would that in some perverse way help you to be less afraid
yourselves, because you are both very afraid, and I find it
distinctly repulsive that you turn together against me for
the sole reason of backing each other up in your fight
against them. We are in this together. Don't forget that. If I
go under, so do you.
(*Silence.*)
ADAM: Shoot the movie.
EDWARD: There were three bollocks in a cell in Lebanon. An
Englishman, an Irishman, and an American. Why they
were in that cell was anybody's guess, and why they were in
Lebanon was their own guess.
ADAM: The American was the first to be caught. While he was
on his own, he was frightened of going mad.
EDWARD: The Irishman was second to be caught. He would
have went mad without the American. They were joined,
these two bolloxes, by a third bollocks, an Englishman.
MICHAEL: The Englishman did not know if being in the cell in
Lebanon had driven the other two mad. What has
happened to him in being kidnapped strikes him as being
madness, so he has attempted not to lose his head in the
face of severe provocation –
EDWARD: In not being afraid of them he's convinced them they
have not gone mad.
ADAM: And in their way, in so far as is possible, they thank him
for that conviction.
(*Silence.*)
MICHAEL: You both scare the shit out of me.

EDWARD: English people always scare the shit out of me as well. As for fucking Americans –

MICHAEL: Yes, they are all quite mad –

EDWARD: Can you imagine what it was like to land in here with that yankee –

MICHAEL: Yes, it must have been worrying –

ADAM: What the fuck is this?

MICHAEL: I do wish we could stop swearing. My language has gone to pot since meeting you both. I really do feel that we are giving in to them if we allow ourselves to descend to vulgarity – no, I'm being a sanctimonious prig. I apologize. (*Silence.*)
I'd also just like to say that I think Richard Attenborough's films are quite good. He spent over twenty years trying to make *Gandhi*, and it's a testimony to his decent, well-crafted and honourable political views –

EDWARD: Michael?

MICHAEL: What?

ADAM: Shite.

MICHAEL: Well, it was a bit long, the film of *Gandhi*. (*Silence.*)

ADAM: I wonder what Sam Peckinpah would have done with the life of Gandhi.

EDWARD: Gandhi would have been shot in the first reel.

MICHAEL: Actually, Gandhi is shot in the first reel of Richard Attenborough's film.

EDWARD: Is that a fact?

MICHAEL: Yes. (*Silence.*)
Are there any vultures in Lebanon?

ADAM: What do you mean?

MICHAEL: Well, in the film where Madonna is eaten by vultures, would that be realistic in Lebanon? (*Silence.*)
That was meant to be a joke. (*Silence.*)
Vultures are much maligned creatures, you know. I'm not an expert myself on their dietary habits, but I did once hear

on *Round Britain Quiz* a fascinating description –
ADAM: Michael, I am Sam Peckinpah. This is a gun.
(*He points his finger at* MICHAEL.)
You are dead.
(*He shoots* MICHAEL.)
EDWARD: What a senseless waste of human life.
MICHAEL: Do you think we'll ever get out of here?
(*Silence.*)
What can they possibly gain by holding us hostage?
(*Silence.*)
My mother isn't terribly well. She'll be very worried about me. Do you think they will have at least let her know I'm alive? I know it may not sound very sensible to be worried about one's mother when we're in the position that we're in, but I do worry, I worry so much – I was just wondering if they would have told her not to worry –
ADAM: I'm sure they have.
EDWARD: Yes.
MICHAEL: Yes.
(*Silence.*)
It is quite worrying, isn't it?
EDWARD: Yes.
MICHAEL: Yes.
ADAM: It's just as well you're not afraid.
(*Silence.*)
MICHAEL: We could be here a long time, couldn't we?
(*Silence.*)
ADAM: That was my major reservation about *Gandhi*. It was too long, that film. Very long.
(*Lights fade.*)

SCENE FOUR

ADAM *rocks himself to and fro, gently, humming 'Someone to Watch Over Me'.* MICHAEL *sits wide awake, alternating his*

gaze from ADAM *to* EDWARD. EDWARD *sleeps.*
EDWARD *mumbles in his sleep.* ADAM *whispers to himself.*

ADAM: Mama and Papa, Mama and Papa, Mama, Papa.
MICHAEL: It's extraordinary how little sleep I need in here. You
 haven't been sleeping terribly well either, Adam.
ADAM: Adam's won a scholarship, Adam's Phi Beta Kappa, are
 you proud of me?
 (ADAM *continues singing 'Someone To Watch Over Me'.*)
MICHAEL: Edward, of course, is dead to the world.
ADAM: No, they were too busy, too many foster kids, got to look
 after the foster kids. We welcome in our house all our
 unfortunate little brothers and sisters. Do your bit to build a
 new America. So they thought, while the rest of America was
 flushing itself down the toilet. And Adam is such a help to
 us.
MICHAEL: How were you a help?
ADAM: Adam is bright. Maybe he's too bright. How could he be
 too bright? Adam worries too much. If we let him, he'd take
 on all our worries. Get rid of your worries, folks, get rid of
 the foster kids. Get rid of the fucking foster kids. Oh God,
 help me. I want to – what do I want? Sleep – just sleep. I
 can't. Because when I sleep, I dream. I dream of my mother
 and my father, and I hear all the fights in that fighting house.
 I dream of my girlfriend. I dream of her family. I dream of
 myself. And I am so scared, because I no longer recognize
 myself in this dream. God help me. God help me. Get me out
 of here. Please, Please. There, there, baby. Be quiet. I'm
 here, I'm here, your Mama's here. She's strong. Your Papa
 loves you. Please keep your sanity, kind, good Adam, we
 need your strength so much.
 (*Silence.*)
MICHAEL: I am sorry to see you in pain. Shall I waken Edward?
ADAM: No.
MICHAEL: I wish he were awake.
ADAM: How long have you been here?
MICHAEL: Four weeks and three days, I'm keeping a count.
ADAM: Do that, yea. The first month you keep counting. And the

second month. In my third month, Edward came. And so you get to know him, fourth month. He gets to know you the next month. Then you want to kill him. Or you want to kill yourself. And the worst month, this month, you don't want them to kill you. What you want is to go home. All the time, want to go home. Want to hear one American, any American voice, apart from your own. How dare you? I'm an American. How dare you do this? I'm an American.

(EDWARD *wakes up.*)

EDWARD: Adam, what the hell is this?

ADAM: How dare you hurt me like this?

EDWARD: What's wrong with him?

MICHAEL: He's an American.

EDWARD: Come on, Adam, come on.

ADAM: What have I done to you?

EDWARD: It's me, it's Ed, it's me. Michael's here. It's us.

(*Silence.*)

You're all right. You're all right.

(*Silence.*)

ADAM: I've got to keep myself looking good.

MICHAEL: You look terribly well, Adam.

(*Silence.*)

ADAM: They won't harm us. We're their most valuable asset.

MICHAEL: I find some consolation in that, you know. When I lost my university post, I did feel redundant. You see, I devoted a large part of my life to building up a department, and hey presto, one wave from the wicked witch's wand, and it's gone. So it's nice to feel valuable. Wanted in some way.

(*Silence.*)

Pathetic, isn't it?

ADAM: What is an American?

EDWARD: Someone born in America.

ADAM: An American is, I repeat, a valuable asset. A prize possession. Prized, yes, valued, but not loved. There is a price permanently placed on the American's head. And *in* his head the American believes the value of the price placed upon him, because his is a market economy, and in that

21

economy everything has a price. But that same market decrees the price may differ in day-to-day dealing. And the valuable asset, the prize possession, this American, has no control over his price. Whoever has no control is fucked. I am American, I am Arab, I am fucked. We have that much in common.

(*Silence.*)

How did your wife die?

MICHAEL: Nita? An accident. Life was different without her.

(*Silence.*)

But Nita certainly would not have wanted me to turn into a weeping willow, so, one got on with sweet life as if, well, nothing happened. Something had happened. Professionally, I changed. Before her death I was full of ideas for publications. Nothing terribly exciting. Mostly on English dialects. Anyway, after the incident, I simply read the Old English elegies and the medieval romances, and I taught as best I could. I published nothing. I'd lost my wife and my ambition. My lack of publications didn't help at the time of the rationalization. Well, these things happen.

EDWARD: That's cheered us all up.

MICHAEL: It wasn't intended to cheer you up. It wasn't even intended for your ears. I was speaking to Adam, who asked me a question. Are you feeling a little better, Adam?

ADAM: No, I hate these shorts.

MICHAEL: There isn't much we can do about that.

ADAM: I want a pair of jockey shorts. I want to wear my country's greatest contribution to mankind. Fresh, white jockey shorts. A man's underwear. That's why Arabs can't wear them. If their shorts don't have a hole in them, they can't find their dicks. I want a pair of jockey shorts. I want to kill an Arab. Just one. Throw his body down before his mother and father, his wife and kids, and say, I did it, me, the American. Now you can blame me. You are justified in what you do to me. You have deserved this. I want to see their faces fill with hate. True hate. I want that within my power.

(*Silence.*)

Fetch me the Koran that I may read of power.

(*He reads from the Koran.*)
In the name of God, the Merciful, the Compassionate.
Behold, we sent it down on the Night of Power:
And what shall teach thee what is the Night of Power?
The Night of Power is better than a thousand months;
In it the angels and the Spirit descend,
By the leave of the Lord, upon every command.
Peace it is, till the rising of dawn.
(*Silence.*)
Peace it is, the Night of Power.
(*Silence.*)
Peace in the house, when the foster kids are sleeping.
Everyone at peace, except Adam in his head. His head is hot.
He forgets his manners. He shoots off his mouth. He hurts.
Forgive me, my sisters and my brothers, for doubting if you
were sisters and brothers. Forgive me, my foes, for calling
you my foes. In your good book lies the way to power and to
peace.
(*He kisses the Koran.*)
I am come into my garden, oh beloved.
Thou that dwellest in the gardens, the companions
hearken to thy voice: cause me to hear it.
Make haste, my beloved, and be thou like to a roe or
to a young hart upon the mountains of spices . . .
Ah but my beloved, why do you turn aside from me?
I am my beloved's, and my beloved is mine.
EDWARD: Well, will we write our letters?
ADAM: Is it time?
MICHAEL: What letters?
ADAM: Home.
MICHAEL: Will they post them? Will they give us pen and paper?
EDWARD: Teach him, Adam.
ADAM: No, you go first. You write to your wife.
EDWARD: Dearest wife, what is your name again? That was a
joke. There is no address at the top of this as I don't know
where I am, but then I never did, as you would say. You
know I'm not a great one for writing letters, but I know
you'd want to hear from me, I hope. I am doing well and

23

bearing up and trust you and our family are doing likewise. There are now two other men with me, Adam the American who is getting married soon and we will be at his wedding if we have to sell the house; and Michael, who is an Englishman. Enough said. I can no more understand why I am here than you can. It is a terrible thing to keep a man or woman from their family when they have done nothing. All right, maybe I was a fool to come to this country, but I wanted to, and you would never stop me – that is why I – that is you all over. Tell the boys to keep supporting Manchester United. Forget Liverpool. Up United. Tell them also their sister is the best footballer of the three of them. And why? Because she is a dirty wee bollocks. Beautiful, but bad. Like her father. I thought I would leave you laughing, and I only wish I could hear you, your husband, Edward.

     P.S. What do you mean, Edward who?

ADAM: That's pretty good, Edward. Michael, you want a go?

MICHAEL: Dear Mum, I am very well. I am sorry that circumstances have prevented me phoning you every Sunday, as promised. I share accommodation with an American and an Irishman and so I am often flooded by a torrent of emotions, which I rise above. The guards who are attending us are terribly distant. The nearest I've met to them are our awful neighbours, the snooty Shawcrosses. Fortunately the Shawcrosses don't carry guns and knives. I hope the new vicar is working out for the best and has abandoned the idea of folk-singing and clog-dancing at the harvest festival. Please don't be tempted to try either. Edward, the Irishman, is interested in soccer. I hope Peterborough United are doing well, for, as you know, I follow soccer as well. I am writing this letter on the first of the month. You always said rabbits on the first of the month. For luck. So, rabbits. For luck. Your loving son, Michael.

     Oh go ahead, Edward. Start straightaway.

EDWARD: Start what?

MICHAEL: Attack me for writing to my mother. Pansy little

Englishman. I don't mind. I've had it before. I can tell you, there were people who were surprised I got married. Look at him sitting there smirking.

EDWARD: I did not open my mouth.

MICHAEL: I read it in your letter. Dear wife, dear children. Support Manchester United. It's enough to make me vomit.

EDWARD: Did I open my mouth against him?

MICHAEL: Sitting there, gloating –

EDWARD: Would you like me to stand up and dance a jig?

MICHAEL: I buried my wife. I can't write to her. I heard that letter. It was an attack on me.

EDWARD: You were far from my mind.

MICHAEL: 'There's an Englishman with us. Enough said.'

EDWARD: You came into this cell –

MICHAEL: It is not a cell. I am in a room. I have never been inside a prison and I never will be. How dare you put me in a cell?

EDWARD: You came into this room then –

MICHAEL: This room, yes.

EDWARD: We tried to help you.

MICHAEL: Help me? How? You throw your wife into my face. You throw your children in my face. I have neither. Yes, you've succeeded. I've failed. That's what you're really saying, isn't it?

EDWARD: Adam, you started this caper, stop it.

MICHAEL: He will not stop it. You mock me for writing to my mother.

EDWARD: Listen, boy, we're sitting together on death row, and what concerns you, stupid bastard? That I'm mocking you, when I have not, you English –

ADAM: Arab? English Arab? Irish Arab? Right, guys? Jesus, these guys don't need to tear us apart. We can tear each other apart.

(*Silence.*)

Can I write my letter now? Is it my turn?

(*Silence.*)

Dear folks, here I am, still in the shit. We have been joined by an English guy, called Michael. Edward is fine. I am bearing up. No, I am not. Forgive me if this upsets you, babes, but you know how I mentioned that I sometimes feel like a hunted animal, even though I am caught in this cage. The hunters seem to be getting closer. I can smell their guns. One night I dreamt that I had died. You were looking down at me. Papa, you reached out to touch my dead body, and when you touched me, I came back to life. I hope this dream comes true. I am going to die. There are nights when I listen to the silence and I think we are all of us going to die. I don't know what I am going to do. The only time we may leave the cell is to go to the toilet. They normally do not let us close the bathroom door. This time the Arab guy slammed the door shut. I stood there for a long time. When they threw open the door, there were three of them, waiting for me. And one raised his hand and pointed his finger at me.

(ADAM *does so.*)

I have been selected to go first. Since this happened, my head has not really been right. Maybe I just imagined this. But I feel that finger pointed at me, and I am very scared. I love you both, Adam.

(*Silence.*)

Guys, what am I going to do? They got my ass over a barrel, and I ain't wearing jockey shorts. I smell oil. They're going to cream my ass with oil, and they're going to fuck me dead. Up my ass, baby. Up my ass. Will they kill me for oil?

(*Silence.*)

So, it's the first of the month, Michael?

EDWARD: I won't let them. They won't kill you.

ADAM: Say rabbits. For luck. Say it.

MICHAEL: Rabbits.

ADAM: Rabbits. For luck. Rabbits. Rabbits.

(*Lights fade.*)

SCENE FIVE

EDWARD *sits wide awake.* ADAM *sits, crouched, humming 'Someone to Watch Over Me', reading the Koran.* MICHAEL *lies sleeping.*

James McDaniel

ADAM: I want a pair of jockey shorts. I want to wear my
    country's greatest contribution to mankind.... I want to kill
    an Arab. Just one. Throw his body down before his mother
    and father, his wife and kids, and say, I did it, me, the
    American. Now you can blame me. You are justified in
    what you do to me.

Photos by Tom Lawlor

Alec McCowen

MICHAEL: Dear Mum, I am very well. I am sorry that circumstances have prevented me phoning you every Sunday, as promised. I share accommodation with an American and an Irishman and so I am often flooded by a torrent of emotions, which I rise above.

Stephen Rea (left) with Alec McCowen.

MICHAEL: My God, it's moving, it's moving. I'm driving a car. I'm actually driving a car. Look at me, driving a car.

EDWARD: Wave to the people, they're cheering you.

(MICHAEL *waves regally*.)

MICHAEL: I'm as drunk as the Queen Mother.

Stephen Rea

EDWARD: There's been darkness in this room. I've felt the
enemy surround me in the dark…. But I want to say this, I
am a better man than any of them, for I would not torture
them like this. That is my choice. They do as they're
ordered. I do as I choose. Locked in chains, for all to see,
but not beaten down to the ground yet. In the Name of
God, the Merciful, the Compassionate.

EDWARD: Wake and sleep, wake and sleep, what else is there to do, eh, Michael? What are you dreaming of? Mammy in Peterborough? Are you dreaming of us, Michael? Are you? (*Silence.*)
Do you feel like a bit of exercise, Adam?
(ADAM *continues humming.*)
Are you still asleep, Michael?

ADAM: In the Name of God, the Merciful, the Compassionate.

EDWARD: Look at him. Sleeping like a big baby. Happy in his nappy. I think he's less cross than when he came in here. Maybe he's stopped teething.

ADAM: In the Name of God, the Merciful, the Compassionate.
We have sent the Koran on thee.
Remember the name of the Lord.
You cry lies like the voice of Doom.
But over you there are watchers,
Over you there are watchers,
Watchers, over you, over you.
We have sent the Koran down on thee,
Remember the name of the Lord.
Say to unbelievers,
I serve not what you serve,
And you are not serving what I serve,
But to you, your religion, and to me my religion.
To you, your religion, to me, my religion.
In the Name of God, the Merciful, the Compassionate.
(*Silence.*)

EDWARD: To you, your religion, and to me, my religion? The Koran?
(*Silence.*)
Save us from all who believe they're right. Right, in the name of God who is not merciful and not compassionate, for he is like them, always right. I've seen it at home before. Scared wee shits, panting with fear, ready to make the big sacrifice. They must be right, for if they're wrong, God help them. And if they're right, God help us. It's the workings of the world I fear, and my fate it is to fear, said the blind man screwing his mother.

27

ADAM: I hope she enjoyed it.
EDWARD: In the name of God the merciful, the compassionate.
ADAM: And if he's not?
EDWARD: Then he's not.
ADAM: What are we going to do then?
(*Silence.*)
What are we going to do?
EDWARD: Be men.
ADAM: And do what?
EDWARD: Face up to your fate.
ADAM: And then what?
EDWARD: Defy it. Defy them. Fight them. Never show pain in front of them.
ADAM: Never.
EDWARD: Never.
(*Silence.*)
ADAM: I think what first started to drive me mad in this place is not knowing what time of day it is. I think it's night.
EDWARD: I know it is.
ADAM: Are you afraid of the dark?
EDWARD: There's been darkness in this room. I've felt the enemy surround me in the dark. Listening, waiting for me to crack, to cry. They think I'm in their power. I am, the three of us are. They decide if we live or die. It's up to them. But there is still one thing left up to me. Me alone. Have they, or have they not, made me less of a man, by reason of what they've done to me? And they haven't. They've made themselves less than men, in locking me away like this. No matter what cause they are doing it for they have still made themselves less than men. But I want to say this, I am a better man than any of them, for I would not torture them like this. That is my choice. They do as they're ordered. I do as I choose. Locked in chains, for all to see, but not beaten down to the ground yet. In the Name of God, the Merciful, the Compassionate.
(*Silence.*)
ADAM: We're at their mercy.
EDWARD: We're at our own.

ADAM: Our fate?

EDWARD: Face it, I said. Face it.

(*Silence.*)

ADAM: Will you be able to look after Michael? He's growing more and more frightened.

EDWARD: He's learning to fight his corner.

ADAM: He won't be able to.

EDWARD: Do you think he was married at all? What did a wife see in him?

ADAM: What did your wife see in you?

EDWARD: More than a drink of water, I can tell you.

ADAM: He'll need you.

EDWARD: Let's stop this chat. Why are you already acting as if you're not here? Wise up, boy. You're still a valuable commodity. We are their prize heifers. You keep the same heifers for display. And rest assured of one thing. If the boys out there bump you off, I won't be long after you at the pearly gates. If I'm left alone with Michael, I'm bumping myself off.

ADAM: Commit suicide? You? Never.

EDWARD: Don't bank on it. You're never been to an NUJ union meeting. The slowest form of suicide known to man.

MICHAEL: Are you talking about suicide?

EDWARD: Were you not sleeping, you bollocks?

MICHAEL: I've just woken up. Were you saying something about suicide?

ADAM: Have you tried it?

MICHAEL: I certainly thought about it after Nita's death. She reasoned me out of it.

EDWARD: You saw her ghost?

MICHAEL: Don't be so ridiculous. There is no such thing as ghosts. I simply had an imaginary conversation with her. As usual, she gave me excellent advice. I did as advised.

ADAM: Which was?

MICHAEL: Make my pear flan. She adored my pear flan.

EDWARD: If I hear one more word about this fucking pear flan –

MICHAEL: Honestly, the Irish have the most attractive accent but their coarseness is so self-defeating. Without it, I do believe they would have the most beautiful dialect of English.

EDWARD: Dialect?

MICHAEL: Hiberno-English can be quite a lovely dialect. Those Elizabethan turns of phrase, those syntactical oddities, which I believe owe something to Gaelic, the sibilants –

EDWARD: You called it a dialect.

MICHAEL: It is a dialect. Hiberno-English.

EDWARD: What I speak is not a dialect of English.

MICHAEL: Then what do you call it? Portuguese?

EDWARD: Call my language what you like. It is not a dialect.

MICHAEL: You are a profoundly ignorant man.

EDWARD: Am I? Listen, times have changed, you English mouth, and I mean mouth. One time when you and your breed opened that same mouth, you ruled the roost, you ruled the world, because it was your language. Not any more. We've taken it from you. We've made it our own. And now, we've bettered you at it. You thought you had our tongues cut out, sitting crying a corner, lamenting. Listen. The lament's over. We took you and your language on, and we won. Not bad for a race that endured eight hundred years of oppression, pal, and I speak as a man who is one generation removed from the dispossessed.

ADAM: Edward, you had a university education. You live in a more than comfortable home. You earn a large salary. How in hell are you dispossessed?

EDWARD: One generation removed, I said. And there are those I hold responsible for that dispossession. Him, being one.

(EDWARD *points at* MICHAEL.)

MICHAEL: There is not much historical validity to that charge.

EDWARD: Remember the Famine? The Great Hunger?

MICHAEL: The Irish Famine was a dreadful event. I don't dispute its seriousness. But I'm sorry. How can I be personally responsible for what happened then? It was a hundred and fifty fucking years ago.

EDWARD: It was yesterday.

MICHAEL: You are ridiculous, Edward.

EDWARD: I am Irish.

MICHAEL: Then may I ask you Irish one question, if I am personally responsible? I am a little troubled by the Famine.

30

Could it be you only had your silly selves to blame?

EDWARD: Adam, I'm going to knife him.

MICHAEL: You left yourselves utterly dependent on the potato. Why didn't you try for a more balanced diet? Carrots are delicious. What about bread and cheese?

EDWARD: Jesus.

MICHAEL: That's typical. That is so Irish. Call on Jesus to solve your problems. Well, what if you had called on Jesus, and he said, 'Turn Protestant'? What would have happened them?

EDWARD: Some of us did turn Protestant.

MICHAEL: And what happened to them?

EDWARD: We ate them without salt.

MICHAEL: Quite nutritious I hope they were too.

ADAM: Guys, give me a break.

MICHAEL: I was provoked. You heard him.

(*Silence.*)

What you accused me of was unfair, but I did say things that were unthinking, as did you, and you did accuse me personally.

EDWARD: I accused you of nothing.

MICHAEL: Adam is my witness. You held me personally responsible for eight hundred years of persecution.

EDWARD: That was a joke. Have you no sense of humour?

MICHAEL: I have an excellent sense of humour.

EDWARD: You have as much sense of humour as my arse.

MICHAEL: Then my sympathies to your arse being stuck with you.

ADAM: Guys, please, guys.

MICHAEL: It's preposterous. He does nothing to alleviate this dreadful situation. There are times I believe he is on their side out there. I have done nothing to offend him. Yet he attacks me, knowing how distressed I am when I don't know if my mother is alive or dead, and I don't know if I'm going to live or die. We could at least maintain the semblance of civility in this dreadful – dreadful . . . Quite preposterous. If your intentions were to annoy me, you have succeeded admirably.

(*Silence.*)

31

I apologize for that dreadful outburst. I may have put us all at risk by that dreadful outburst.

(*Silence.*)

I have said some very stupid things.

(*Silence.*)

EDWARD: I was stupid.

MICHAEL: Selfish. As I was. We're not thinking of Adam.

EDWARD: Adam's fine.

MICHAEL: Of course Adam is, but if Adam wishes to complain –

EDWARD: Adam will.

MICHAEL: Adam is too –

ADAM: Hey, fuckers, Adam's here. He can speak for himself.

MICHAEL: Of course you can, Adam.

EDWARD: Right you be, Adam.

ADAM: So shut it. For as long as you are here, I am here. OK?

(*Silence.*)

MICHAEL: It would be wonderful to be released together, wouldn't it? You must promise to come to Peterborough and see the cathedral. I do believe it is the most glorious building in all of England. When I was a boy I really did think God lived in it.

EDWARD: Good enough football team, Peterborough United.

MICHAEL: Edward, they've never been out of the fourth division.

EDWARD: One year they made the third. Kicked out, weren't they, some scandal over money?

MICHAEL: We don't talk about it.

EDWARD: I'm still surprised you're a supporter.

MICHAEL: One has a certain loyalty.

EDWARD: Yes, I know. Dear old dirty Dublin. When you come there, I'll take you round it on the Dart. It's a train that runs along the coast of Dublin, from Howth to Bray. Howth to Bray. Raheny, Harmonstown, Connolly, Tara, Sandymount, Booterstown, Booterstown – Jesus, to see those names, to say them. There's a bird sanctuary at Booterstown. Kingfishers fly there. I saw one once. I pointed it out to my daughter.

(*Silence.*)

Can you remember birds singing?

(*Silence.*)

The Birdman of Alcatraz, that was a great film, wasn't it?

ADAM: Alcatraz is near my home. When I take you to San Francisco, to Fremont, we'll cross the bay and go to Chinatown, where they have the best fish restaurants in America. Lobster, lobster, and more lobster.
(*Silence.*)
It's going to be OK.
(*Silence.*)
It's all going to be OK.

MICHAEL: Do you know that no one has ever precisely explained the etymology of OK?

EDWARD: My, have they not?

MICHAEL: My favourite theory is the Stonewall Jackson one. You may have heard this, Adam. It concerns the American Civil War –

EDWARD: A lot of Irishmen died in that war.

MICHAEL: Mostly fighting to retain slavery.

EDWARD: Give me proof of that.

MICHAEL: *Gone with the Wind.*

EDWARD: What?

MICHAEL: With a name like Scarlett O'Hara she was hardly from Knightsbridge.

ADAM: Just give us the Stonewall Jackson theory, Michael.

MICHAEL: It's said he never learned to read or write, so when he got papers to sign, he always put OK at the bottom, because he spelt all with an 'o' and correct with a 'k'.

EDWARD: Couldn't read or write, could he?

MICHAEL: So they say.

EDWARD: Completely illiterate then, was he?

MICHAEL: That would follow, yes.

EDWARD: If somebody is completely illiterate not merely can they not spell, they also cannot mis-spell. If he couldn't read or write how would he know about an 'o' or 'k'?

MICHAEL: Yes. That shatters the Stonewall Jackson theory somewhat.

EDWARD: It does, somewhat.

MICHAEL: Theory is so dangerous in all academic matters. Now take lingusitics itself –

EDWARD: What have I stated?

MICHAEL: I lost interest years ago in modern linguistics. All that heated debate over the Bloomfield/Chomsky controversy. It's all so dated now. Chomsky's theories themselves –

EDWARD: Have disappeared up their own arse.

MICHAEL: Yes, they have, actually.

(*Silence.*)

EDWARD: I'd love a cigarette. I'd love a drink.

MICHAEL: I could murder a cup of tea.

(*Silence.*)

EDWARD: Fuck it, I'm breaking out, I'm having a drink. Anybody joining me? Adam, first shout, what do you want to drink?

ADAM: A beer.

EDWARD: How about a little Martini?

ADAM: A vodka Martini then.

EDWARD: Twist or olive, sir?

ADAM: Twist *and* olive. I'm a mean vodka Martini man.

EDWARD: Michael, what are you having?

MICHAEL: Just a sherry, please.

EDWARD: A sherry? All right. Sweet sherry?

MICHAEL: Medium, please.

EDWARD: One small medium sherry coming up.

MICHAEL: Oh, what the heck – make it a large one.

EDWARD: Yes, what the heck.

ADAM: Hey, do I detect the fragrance of an exotic substance passing from hand to hand through this distinguished company? Pass it here. And I'll have another vodka Martini.

EDWARD: Coming up, sir. And I'll have the same. Cheers. (*Roars.*) Hold it. Quiet.

MICHAEL: What is it?

EDWARD: Listen. Do you hear. Close your eyes. You'll hear it. The door, it's opening. Somebody's coming in.

(*Silence.*)

It's them. They've heard us enjoying ourselves. They know we're drinking. Keep your eyes closed. They're here. They're watching us. They're angry. Do you see them?

(*Silence.*)

34

They don't approve of this. They're going to stop us. What
are we going to do?
(*Silence.*)
ADAM: Drink.
(*Silence.*)
EDWARD: Drink?
MICHAEL: Drink.
EDWARD: Drink.
(*They down the imaginary drinks.*)
We haven't done as we're told. We've got them in a state of
shock. They're ours for the taking. What will we do with
them? Look, boys, at this. A full keg of Guinness. Enough to
drown a man. Will I drown them with drink? Will I drown
them? Will I?
(*Silence.*)
MICHAEL: It would be rather a waste of the Guinness.
EDWARD: Good man, Michael, you said it. So will we let them sit
down? Will we make space for them? Do you invite them to
the party?
(ADAM *nods.*)
Take the weight off your feet, boys. Imagine it's a wedding,
or as near as makes no difference. Bit of a song. A story. The
same the world over. Have a drink if you like. We won't tell.
Join us.
ADAM: Will they?
EDWARD: Up to them. In the Name of God, the Merciful, the
Compassionate. To you, your religion, and to me, what?
What to me? To the happy day I'm let go, alive. Cheers,
men. Just for the night, celebrate. Come on. Will you join
us?
MICHAEL: What are they going to do?
EDWARD: Staying. They love a song,. Arabs. They've heard we're
great singers.
(EDWARD *sings 'The Water Is Wide'*:)
   The water is wide, and I can't cross o'er,
   And neither have I wings to fly.
   Give me a boat that can carry two,
   And both shall row, my love and I.

35

For love is gentle and love is kind,
And love is sweet when first it's new,
But love grows old and waxes cold
And fades away like morning dew.

There is a ship and its sails the sea,
She's loaded deep, as deep can be,
But not as deep as the love I'm in
I know not how I sink or swim.
(ADAM *joins Edward in the song.*)

ADAM *and* EDWARD: The water is wide, and I can't cross o'er,
    And neither have I wings to fly.
    Give me a boat, that can carry two,
    And both shall row, my love and I.
    (*At the song's conclusion,* MICHAEL *rattles the chains,* EDWARD
    and ADAM *following suit. Suddenly there is silence.*)

EDWARD: It's quiet back there. The Arab boys must have slipped
    out.

MICHAEL: Did they enjoy themselves?

EDWARD: They didn't say.

MICHAEL: Their rudeness takes my breath away.

EDWARD: These boys never say anything. Their strength depends
    on silence. Careless talk costs lives. That's scrawled on every
    wall from Belfast to Derry. The nearest I ever really came to
    anything like the same boys, I was driving to Newry, there
    had been some other outrage and, foolish man, I stopped to
    give this, what I thought was a down-and-out, a lift. He got
    into the car, and then I saw he was carrying a rucksack. I said
    nothing about the rucksack, I tried to make general
    conversation, but no go. Not a word out of him but yes or
    no. I finally asked him, what's in the rucksack? He looked at
    me and he said, mind your own fucking business. The sweat
    started to break out on me. We were coming near to a police
    checkpoint, so I stopped the car and asked him again about
    the rucksack. Mind your own fucking business, that was his
    reply. I said, get you and your rucksack out of my car. He
    opened the door, run like hell, and left the rucksack lying

there. The sweat was now blinding me. I opened – I opened the rucksack. I opened it.

MICHAEL: What was in the rucksack?

EDWARD: Mind your own fucking business.

(*They laugh lowly,* MICHAEL *still looking confused.*)

MICHAEL: Edward, what was in the rucksack?

EDWARD: Michael, it's a joke.

MICHAEL: Oh I get it, I get it. There was nothing at all in the rucksack. Very good. (*Laughs.*) Very amusing, Edward.

EDWARD: Time for the story. Mick, you're in the good form. Tell it.

MICHAEL: There's a terribly sad story in Old English. It's a poem, called 'The Wanderer'.

EDWARD: We want a happy story.

MICHAEL: There's a very happy story in Middle English called 'Sir Orfeo'. It's really based on Ovid's Orpheus myth, and the variations from the classical sources reveal the essential optimism of the medieval mind and its profound faith in human happiness to triumph over despair. I find that mind so much deeper than Renaissance doubt. It can be so destructive at times, doubt. It has its place, lack of faith, and I myself suffer from it at times –

EDWARD: Are you going to tell us the story?

MICHAEL: Long ago there lived a knight called Sir Orfeo who married a lady called Herodis, and they loved each other. They lived in England, in Winchester, actually. Medieval poets tend to set the ancient myths in familiar places. Part of their charm. Where was I? Yes, Herodis was full of love and goodness, no man could describe her fairness. One day Herodis slept under the shade of a magical tree and to cut a long story short, she was stolen by death who came to her as a king, the King of the Underworld.

EDWARD: Did he live in Winchester as well?

MICHAEL: The Isle of Wight, actually. Don't be facetious. She was stolen by death. Orfeo, who, by the way, was a great musician, wept for his wife and went into the forest, there to lead a living death, for he knew whither thou goest, I will go with thee, and whither I go, thou shalt go with me . . . Yes,

yes . . . He entered hell and played music, and won back his
wife, and returned safely to Winchester. Thus came Sir
Orfeo out of his care. God grant us all as well to fare.
Amen.

EDWARD: Very nice, Michael.

ADAM: Really great.

MICHAEL: Is there any more drink?

EDWARD: Sherry?

MICHAEL: I think I'll try a vodka Martini.

EDWARD: Three vodka Martinis coming up. Catch, lads.
Cheers.

ADAM: Cheers.

MICHAEL: Indeed. Quite delicious.
(*Silence.*)

EDWARD: So, Adam, you're being quiet. A quiet man.
(ADAM *sings.*)

ADAM: Amazing grace, how sweet it sounds,
That saved a wretch like me.
I once was lost but now am found,
Was blind, but now I see.

Through many dangers, tall and stern
We have already come.
We have this day to sing God's praise,
Than when we first begun.

Amazing grace, how sweet it sounds,
That saved a wretch like me.
I once was lost, but now I'm found,
Was blind, but now I see.
(*Silence.*)

MICHAEL: Thank you.

EDWARD: Thank you.

ADAM: Thank you.
(*Lights fade.*)

SCENE SIX

MICHAEL *is eating his meal from a bowl.* EDWARD *lets his food sit untouched beside him. The chain that held* ADAM *lies empty.*

MICHAEL: This is good.
(*He eats more in silence.*)
It's chicken. The vegetables are fresh as well. A bit overcooked for me. Undercooked for you, I'd say. But it's good.
(*Silence.*)
Aren't you going to eat? You must be hungry.
(*Silence.*)
You haven't eaten for three days. They're getting worried about you not eating.
(*Silence.*)
This not talking, this not eating, isn't going to help us. We are in a decidedly perilous position, to put it mildly. You might say, put nothing mildly. But we can't push them too far. Push them as far as we can push them, is that it? Then they are liable to turn very nasty indeed. They are in quite a state as it stands. They know what they have done. At the moment they are hovering between apology and arrogance. Trying very hard as I am to take some rational – some comfort out of this, I do feel they themselves did not wish to kill Adam –
He is dead. I have evidence of that, as have you. My evidence is that one of them actually wept –
(*Silence.*)
That's an act he was putting on to mock us, is that what you think? One of them wept when he came into this – this cell. There is no point in believing that. That's a lie? A complete lie? Don't fall for that, yes? They have him in hiding somewhere else? Your main worry is that he may be on his own. He did manage on his own when they first got him. He will manage now. But you are not eating until he is brought back here to us? He is not dead? You firmly believe that. Nothing I can say will convince you otherwise? Do I understand you?

39

(*Silence.*)

EDWARD: They would not kill him.

MICHAEL: What would he have done to stop them?

(*Silence.*)

Adam is dead, Edward.

EDWARD: You want him dead. You feel safer with him dead. One of us down, and no more to go. With him dead there'll be a big outcry and we will be saved. Isn't that it? Well, listen, get that out of your head, for if they've put him down, they can put us down as well. Dogs together, to be shot. Take no consolation from imagining him dead. It won't save you. It won't save me.

MICHAEL: No, it won't save you. You hope it might save you, but you're perfectly correct, his death won't save you. You condemn yourself out of your own mouth. It isn't me who wants him dead. It's you, isn't it?

(*Silence.*)

I don't blame you for thinking that. You want to give his death some – some sense of sacrifice. You are in grief, in mourning. And you are mad with grief.

EDWARD: He is not –

MICHAEL: (*Roars:*) Dead, he is, and you know it.

EDWARD: You know nothing.

MICHAEL: I know about grief. About mourning. How it can destroy you. I know.

(*Silence.*)

You know he's dead, don't you?

(*Silence.*)

Say it, he is dead.

(*Silence.*)

EDWARD: He died. I needed him. Jesus, I needed him.

(*Silence.*)

How could he leave me? How could he do this? Without him, how will I get through this?

MICHAEL: Bury him.

(*Silence.*)

Remember him.

(*Silence.*)

What was he like?

EDWARD: He was gentle. He was kind. He could be cruel, when
he was afraid, and while he was often afraid, as we all are
afraid, he was not often cruel. He was brave, he could
protect himself, and me, and you. He was beautiful to look
at. I watched him as he slept one night I couldn't sleep. He
moved that night through his sleep like a man not dreaming
of what life had in store for him. He was innocent. Kind,
gentle. Friend. I believe it goes without saying, love, so I
never said. He is dead. Bury him. Perpetual light shine upon
him. May his soul rest in peace. Amen.

(*Silence.*)

MICHAEL: Love bade me welcome: yet my soul drew back,
    Guiltie of dust and sinne.
But quick-ey'd Love, observing me grow slack
From my first entrance in,
Drew nearer to me, sweetly questioning,
If I lack'd anything.

A guest, I answer'd, worthy to be here:
Love said, You shall be he.
I the unkinde, ungratefull? Ah my deare,
I cannot look on thee.
Love took my hand, and smiling did reply,.
Who made the eyes but I?

Truth Lord, but I have marr'd them: Let my shame
Go where it doth deserve.
And know you not, sayes Love, who bore the blame?
My deare, then I will serve.
You must sit down, sayes Love, and taste my meat:
So I did sit and eat.

(*Silence.*)

EDWARD: I'm hungry.
MICHAEL: Then eat.
EDWARD: Dear friend.
    (EDWARD *eats.*)
    He's dead.

41

MICHAEL: We are not.
(*Lights fade.*)

MICHAEL *is looking from side to side.* EDWARD *watches him.*
MICHAEL *claps his hands.* EDWARD *remains silent.* MICHAEL *gasps.*
He resumes looking from side to side. He applauds again.

MICHAEL: Great shot.
EDWARD: More fool me for asking, but what the hell are you
   doing?
MICHAEL: Ssh, I'm in the middle of a very important rally.
   (*Jumps to his feet applauding.*) Oh well played, Virginia, well
   played.
   Now they're changing ends I can answer your question. I am
   reliving the 1977 Wimbledon Ladies' Final. Virginia Wade
   of Great Britain against Betty Stove of Holland. The Queen
   in her Silver Jubilee Year is attending Wimbledon for the
   first time. The poor dear is bored to distraction, but Virginia
   is going for a British win and the excitement is mounting.
   Excuse me, the third set is about to continue. I'm going to
   serve.
   (MICHAEL *starts to play a tennis match.*)
   A perfect ace. Virginia is really getting on top of things now.
   What do you think, Dan Maskell? I'm not counting any
   chickens before they're hatched, but I think we should be
   practising a few bars of 'For She's a Jolly Good Fellow'. Oh I
   say, a wonderful shot. Come on, Virginia. Oh dear. He who
   hesitates, or in this case, she who hesitates, can lose all. Oh I
   say, another winner from Virginia.
EDWARD: For the love of Jesus.
MICHAEL: What do you mean, 'for the love of Jesus'?
EDWARD: What are you up to?
MICHAEL: Do I complain when you relive great horse races the
   Irish won? Great football games? Great rugby? I enter the
   spirit of things. Cheer along. So should you.

EDWARD: I'm just feeling sorry for poor wee Betty Stove.

MICHAEL: Poor wee Betty Stove is six foot and weighs twelve stones.

EDWARD: Her mother still thought of her as poor wee Betty.

MICHAEL: Her mother is irrelevant. Virginia is playing to win and is going to win.

EDWARD: That's unfair.

MICHAEL: That's history.

EDWARD: To hell with history, I'm rooting for Betty. Who's serving?

MICHAEL: I am.

EDWARD: Take it away, Virginia.

(MICHAEL *goes to serve, tossing back his head four times.*) What are you doing?

MICHAEL: It's a tense moment in the match. Virginia always tossed her head at a tense moment.

EDWARD: It's distracting.

MICHAEL: It's a habit.

EDWARD: It's a bad habit. You shouldn't . . .

(MICHAEL *suddenly serves.*)

MICHAEL: Another ace. My game.

EDWARD: What do you mean? I wasn't ready.

MICHAEL: My game.

EDWARD: I wasn't ready. I appeal to the umpire. What should I do, Adam?

(*He looks to the empty chair. Silence.* EDWARD *suddenly adopts a loud American voice.*)

You cannot be serious. You cannot be serious. Are you blind? Are you stupid? This is the pits. God damn it.

MICHAEL: I think you'll find John McEnroe was not involved in the 1977 Ladies' Final.

EDWARD: What do you mean? I'm Betty Stove and I was just asking a question. Can you give me an answer? I'm only asking . . .

MICHAEL: A little-known fact about Virginia Wade is that in her youth she was a boxing champion. She applies a neat one–two to Miss Stove and sends her spinning. This is the first Wimbledon Final ever to be settled on a knock-out. Virginia

has done it. Virginia has won Wimbledon. Virginia will have
tea with the Queen. Your majesty.
(MICHAEL *curtsies*.)
EDWARD: What?
MICHAEL: Your majesty. Present me with the award and say
something.
EDWARD: I'm now the Queen?
MICHAEL: Yes.
EDWARD: Hello.
MICHAEL: Hello.
EDWARD: Here you are.
MICHAEL: Thank you.
EDWARD: And what do you do?
MICHAEL: What do you mean, what do I do? You've just seen me
win Wimbledon.
EDWARD: Oh yes, it was very nice.
MICHAEL: Thank you.
EDWARD: You must sweat a lot playing tennis.
MICHAEL: I must, yes.
EDWARD: Is this your racket? It's quite sweaty, I like a little
sweat.
MICHAEL: The Queen is not into sweat.
EDWARD: Why not? The smell of sweat is a well-known turn-on.
MICHAEL: That's enough! Can I have my racket back?
EDWARD: With pleasure.
MICHAEL: Ah, I'm exhausted after those three tough sets.
EDWARD: Yes, you must be.
(*Silence*.)
MICHAEL: You're quite a hairy man, Edward. I've just noticed
that. Have you ever tried the chiffon scarf test?
EDWARD: Immac?
MICHAEL: Ah, you're old enough to remember Immac Hair
Remover? A friend of mine was quite disturbed by his body
hair. So when he read about Immac he bought some in his
local chemist. He told the lady behind the counter it was for
his mother. It worked, the Immac. But when he tried the
chiffon scarf test – you know, shave one leg with a razor, use
Immac on the other leg, the chiffon scarf ought to fall off the

Immac leg, but it didn't on this occasion. He hadn't let the
Immac set. It stuck to his legs, the scarf. The screams were
dreadful. This is true. It did happen to a friend of mine.
EDWARD: What age were you when this happened?
MICHAEL: Seventeen, I'm ashamed to say. How did you know it
was me?
(*Silence.* MICHAEL *sings:*)
Run, Rabbit, run, Rabbit,
Run, run, run,
Here comes the farmer with his big gun,
He'll get by without his rabbit pie,
So run, Rabbit, run, Rabbit,
Run, run, run.
(*Silence.*)
It's actually quite fun if one of us pretends to be the rabbit.
(*Silence.*)
Shall I be the rabbit and you sing?
(*Silence.*)
EDWARD: Run, Rabbit, run, Rabbit,
Run, run, run –
(MICHAEL *scurries about on his chain.*)
What the hell are you doing?
MICHAEL: I'm impersonating a rabbit.
EDWARD: You don't look remotely like a rabbit.
MICHAEL: You could do better?
EDWARD: Sing the song.
(MICHAEL *sings as* EDWARD *impersonates a rabbit:*)
MICHAEL: Run, Rabbit, run, Rabbit,
Run, run, run,
Here comes the farmer with his big gun,
He'll get by without his rabbit pie,
So run, Rabbit, run, Rabbit,
Run, run, run.
EDWARD: Now what's what I call a rabbit.
MICHAEL: You looked more to me like a kangaroo.
EDWARD: How the hell did it look like a kangaroo?
(MICHAEL *impersonates* EDWARD *impersonating a rabbit.*)
MICHAEL: Run Rabbit, run, Rabbit,

45

Run, run, run –

EDWARD: I did not look remotely like that.

MICHAEL: You did, you know it was ridiculous.

EDWARD: I did not start this ridiculous business in the first place.

MICHAEL: No, no, you didn't.

(*Silence.*)

EDWARD: When I was covering the troubles at home I
interviewed this Derry woman. She'd had her windows
broken, I asked her in my innocence – I was a cub reporter –
to sum up the situation. She said, 'Son, this whole situation
can be summed up in two words. Ridiculous, Ridiculous.'

MICHAEL: Is it really our fault for your troubles at home? Is it the
English people's fault?

EDWARD: Ridiculous.

MICHAEL: Is it our fault we're here in the first place?

EDWARD: Ridiculous.

MICHAEL: Do those children holding us captive have a reason to
hate us?

EDWARD: Ridiculous.

MICHAEL: Sum up our situation in two words.

EDWARD: Christ, help us.

MICHAEL: That's three words.

EDWARD: Jesus, look down on us.

MICHAEL: Five words.

EDWARD: God and his blessed mother, help us.

MICHAEL: Ridiculous.

EDWARD: Yes.

MICHAEL: Ridiculous.

(*Silence.*)

EDWARD: They think we have no faith, the Arabs. They are
ridiculous.

MICHAEL: And have we faith?

EDWARD: Do you want proof?

MICHAEL: Yes. Give it to me.

EDWARD: Who won the 1977 Wimbledon Women's Final?

MICHAEL: An Englishwoman won it.

EDWARD: I rest my case that there is a God.

MICHAEL: Well done, Virginia.

46

EDWARD: Well done, Virginia.

MICHAEL: Poor wee Betty Stove.

EDWARD: There always has to be a loser. In every game, a loser.

MICHAEL: Yes, that's history.

(EDWARD *sings:*)

EDWARD: For she's a jolly good fellow,
    For she's a jolly good fellow,
    For she's a jolly good fellow,
    Which nobody can deny.

(*Lights fade.*)

SCENE EIGHT

EDWARD *is exercising strenuously.* MICHAEL *exercises less
strenuously.*

    EDWARD *belts out a song.*

EDWARD: Jingle bells, jingle bells,
    Jingle all the way.

(MICHAEL *breathlessly sings.*)

MICHAEL: Oh what fun it is to ride
    On a one-horse open sleigh.

EDWARD: Hurrah for dear old Santa Claus,
    Hurrah for Christmas Day.

(*Silence.*)

MICHAEL: I'm finding it a little easier now to do ten push-ups.

EDWARD: Good for you.

MICHAEL: I do find I'm growing a little fitter. Isn't it dreadful the
    way a sedentary job ruins the body?

(EDWARD *exercises frantically. He suddenly stops.*)

EDWARD: You're sure it's Christmas Day?

MICHAEL: Nearly certain.

EDWARD: Is it day or night?

MICHAEL: I can't tell.

EDWARD: We should be safe on Christmas Day, even if they don't
    celebrate it.

MICHAEL: Yes, of course.

47

EDWARD: I'm getting out of here. I'm leaving.
MICHAEL: You can't. You're chained to the wall, Edward.
(*Silence.*)
I can guess what's coming now. You're going to get
thoroughly silly and totally upset. Please, do not mention
your family. It won't make things any easier for either of us if
you do insist on remembering them.
(*Silence.* EDWARD *sings.*)
EDWARD: Oh come all ye faithful,
    Joyful and triumphant,
    Oh come ye, oh come ye, to Bethlehem.
(*Silence.*)
And in the manger is the Christ child. Who has caused all
this bother for us. Do you realize that? If we'd been born
Muslims, this wouldn't have happened. So it's his fault. Or
our father's fault and our mother's fault for believing in him.
(EDWARD *sings.*)
    Oh come all ye faithful,
    Joyful and triumphant,
    Oh come ye, oh come ye, to Bethlehem.
(*Silence.*)
Passing the time on a Christmas Day. Peace on earth, good
will to all men. Peace, what's peace, Michael?
(*Silence.*)
Peace is lying beside a woman. Touching her, by accident,
all soft. Smelling her, not stinking like us. Listening to her
breathing. That's the only sound she makes, in the peace.
Her breath. Listen, listen. Peace together, as she sleeps, and
me awake, lovely, lovely. I would press against her belly, and
kiss, and I would be happy as a lark. Her legs move as she
sleeps and I hold them, and want to lift them and conceive in
the morning, on Christmas Day in the morning, in the
happy, happy bed, our bed. Wife. Wife. But who's here but
you, Michael?
(EDWARD *laughs.*)
There are times the sight and sound of you disgust me. I can
feel a smell off you. Sickening. The sight of you sickens me.
The sound of you. I find your smell sickening.

48

MICHAEL: Did you sleep with Adam?
(*Silence.*)
Did you?
EDWARD: No.
MICHAEL: Did you want to?
(*Silence.*)
EDWARD: No.
(*Silence.*)
Do you believe me?
MICHAEL: You didn't have the chance. If you had the chance, if
you hadn't been chained, if I hadn't been here, would you
have slept with him?
(*Silence.*)
If you had known he was going to die, would you have slept
with him?
(*Silence.*)
Beautiful to look at. Kind, gentle.
EDWARD: No. I would not have slept with him.
(*Silence.*)
I would like another child. I want another child.
MICHAEL: Yes.
EDWARD: I need to be a father to my children.
MICHAEL: Yes.
EDWARD: What if I don't come out alive? Anything can happen. I
smoked over forty cigarettes a day before these shites got me.
I could have cancer. Don't laugh at me. It's curable, even
lung cancer, if they get it in time. My Da died from it, and
there's no doctors here. You see, Adam was my great
security. If there had been anything wrong with me, he had
the doctor's gift of the gab. I trusted him. He would tell
them I was a sick man. I need to go home. I was planning
that at Christmas. I want to go home, Michael. It's
Christmas Day. I want to be at home.
MICHAEL: My father was absent at Christmas. For many years.
He was a prisoner, during the war. He returned as a
stranger.
(*Silence.*)
He remained a stranger, poor man. He would never talk

49

about the war. It was not his way to talk. He died, he died
because of the suffering he'd endured during the war. I could
never tell him to me he was a hero. That suffering, his
suffering, was not for nothing. But my father – to know my
father – to love my father –
(MICHAEL *avoids* EDWARD'*s gaze.*)
Would you excuse me?
EDWARD: I will, yes.
(*Silence.*)
MICHAEL: Sometimes they talked quietly about the war, or my
mother did rather. How very frightened people were, but
couldn't show it. Bred into us, that, I suppose. Don't show
fear, even if you're a coward. I never cried as a child, I still
don't cry . . . Yes, yes. One night, out of the blue, I'd fallen
asleep, and I woke up on my father's lap. He was weeping in
front of my mother, and he was saying to her, you must not
tell him what it was like there, you must never tell him. And
I felt the most terrible pain in my ear. I thought my head was
going to explode with pain. I kept on listening, although
even then I knew he was telling her something about the war,
the camp I presume, and I should not have heard anything.
He kept saying her name, her name, repeating it, all the
time. I said, I am awake and I have a pain in my ear. He
rubbed my ear. He said, there is a place called Sparta. Brave
soldiers come from there. When they have pain, they show it
by controlling it. Don't be afraid of pain. Don't be afraid of
controlling it. You have been raised by a strong woman. The
bravest men sometimes behave like women. Before the
Spartans went into battle, they combed each other's hair.
The enemy laughed at them for being effeminate. But the
Spartans won the battle. That was really the only
conversation we ever had. I was old enough to remember
every word.
(*Silence.*)
I did have one other conversation with him. It was after his
death. I was reading an Old English poem called 'The
Wanderer'. A man sits alone in a desolate, frozen landscape,
remembering when he had friends, when he had dreams, and

now he is deserted. And I heard my father. I heard his faith.
And I heard him in that ancient poem, speaking with the
voice of England, talking to itself, for the first time. Our
beginning, our end, England's. One line haunts me. *Oft him
anhaga are gebideth.* I've tried for so long to understand it
fully. I think it means, 'A man who is alone may at times feel
mercy, mercy towards himself.'
(*Silence.*)
We long for our dear life, lamenting great loss – my father is
dead – but accepting fate. *Wyrd bith ful araed.* In the same
poem. *Wyrd bith ful araed.* Fate is fate. When I read 'The
Wanderer', I feel possessed by my father. I feel for him, and
for England. I love my country because I love its literature
very much. I am proud to have taught it. That pride and,
yes, I mean pride, is the reason I can sustain my sanity here.
Most loved mother, remember me . . . most loved missed
father, pray for me . . . most loved missed wife, most loved
wife . . . Rather me were to lose my life, than thus to lose . . .
wife. Ridiculous. Her death was ridiculous.
(MICHAEL *laughs.*)

EDWARD: What happened to her?

MICHAEL:, Ridiculous.

EDWARD: How did she die?

MICHAEL: A car crash. She was driving to work. It was the month
of May. I wasn't with her. I was revising an article at home. I
answered the phone and the university told me she was
unconscious, at the scene of the accident. I knew. I sat by the
phone. Half an hour later they rang to say she was dead. I
went to identify her. She looked like a child who'd fallen off
her bike. It was me persuaded her to buy a car. We were
both working. We could afford a car. Full of love and
goodness. Gone. Such is life. I slept for some time afterwards
with the bedroom light on. Then one night I switched off the
light. Gone. Happy Christmas, Edward.

EDWARD: Happy Christmas, Michael.

MICHAEL: I never learned to drive.

EDWARD: I'm not fucking surprised, sunshine.

MICHAEL: Cherry little soul, am I not?

EDWARD: What do you want for Christmas?

MICHAEL: I'm being given a present?

EDWARD: Anything you want, sir.

MICHAEL: Well, I actually could do with a face flannel.

EDWARD: I don't believe this.

MICHAEL: It's most inconvenient without one.

EDWARD: We've had the shits in this hole, we've no contact with any belonging to us, we have nothing – I'm offering you the world on a plate, and what do you ask for? A face flannel.

MICHAEL: I'm a man of simple tastes. I don't ask for much.

EDWARD: Well, for being a good boy, I'm going to give you something special. Look, it's a car.

MICHAEL: This is in dreadfully bad taste, Edward.

EDWARD: A new car. Hop into it.

MICHAEL: I've hopped.

EDWARD: Switch on the ignition.

MICHAEL: Roger. What now?

EDWARD: The best way to teach someone to drive is to let them find their way into it at their own pace. What do you think you do next?

MICHAEL: I put my foot down on the little thingy.

EDWARD: Put your foot down on the little thingy.

MICHAEL: And I steer with the steerymajig?

EDWARD: The steerymajig.

MICHAEL: And if I want to go faster I press this little fellow?

EDWARD: You do.

MICHAEL: And I release it to drive slower?

EDWARD: You do.

MICHAEL: My God, it's moving, it's moving. I'm driving a car. I'm actually driving a car. Look at me, driving a car.

EDWARD: Wave to the people, they're cheering you.

(MICHAEL *waves regally*.)

MICHAEL: I'm as drunk as the Queen Mother.

EDWARD: I don't want to alarm the Queen Mother, but look behind you. You'll see we're being followed.

MICHAEL: Who by?

EDWARD: The enemy. Drive like hell, they're firing guns.

MICHAEL: Do I press the little fellow?

52

EDWARD: Press, press, press. They're gaining on us.

MICHAEL: I'm pressing, I'm pressing.

EDWARD: Go for it, man. Faster, faster. Think of Steve McQueen in *The Great Escape*.

MICHAEL: What did he do?

EDWARD: He got caught. Fuck him. Forget Steve McQueen. Just go faster.

MICHAEL: Oh my God, Edward, I can't control the steerymajig. It's taking over me. It's got a life of its own. We've got to go where it takes us. Will I keep my foot on the thingy?

EDWARD: Keep your foot on the thingy.

MICHAEL: Edward, the car's started to fly. It's flying. We're in a flying car.

EDWARD: How can a car fly?

(MICHAEL *sings*.)

MICHAEL: Oh you, Chitty-Chitty Bang-Bang,
Chitty-Chitty Bang-Bang we love you,
And our Chitty-Chitty Bang-Bang,
Chitty-Chitty Bang-Bang loves us too.

(EDWARD *joins in*.)

BOTH: Heigh-ho, everywhere we go,
On Chitty-Chitty wheels we say,
Bang-Bang Chitty-Chitty Bang-Bang,
Our fine four-fendered friend,
Bang-Bang Chitty-Chitty Bang-Bang,
Our fine four-fendered friend.

MICHAEL: Whee!

EDWARD: Where are we?

MICHAEL: Flying over the sea. We're leaving this place behind us. Look, Edward, it's Europe. I can see France, and Germany, and Italy. Oh, doesn't Europe look so lovely? Hello, Europe, how are you? Did you miss us? Look, Edward. Down below. It's England. You can see the coast of England. I believe it's Dover. And there are bluebirds over the white cliffs of Dover.

EDWARD: I know. One's just crapped on your head.

MICHAEL: I don't mind. And up north we travel from Dover. Passing London. Why, there's the Houses of Parliament and

53

all who dwell in them, who've left me to rot in a cell in Lebanon. Shall I crap on them, or shall I not waste a good crap? I shall drive on. I can see the spire I'm looking for. Down we go, Chitty. Come on, Edward. We're going to Peterborough. Do you see the cathedral? I'm going to do something I've always wanted to do. I'm going to let Chitty drive to the very top of the cathedral and look down on it from inside the roof.

EDWARD: No, you're not.

MICHAEL: Yes, I am. It's very daring climbing to the rooftop. The public normally aren't even allowed on the third level.

EDWARD: Get me down, I've no head for heights.

MICHAEL: Look at the wonderful west front. The hand of God. Glorious architecture. I do apologize for the stained glass. Victorian. Awful. Well, pretty in their own way, but I'm being generous.

EDWARD: Get me down.

MICHAEL: Don't panic. You're in safe hands. I had a terrible fear of driving, but you taught me to conquer it, and with you in the car beside me, I feel quite safe.

EDWARD: I've news for you. I can't drive either.

(MICHAEL *screams*.)

MICHAEL: We're falling. We're falling.

EDWARD: Keep turning the steerymajig, keep your foot on the thingy.

MICHAEL: I've got my foot on it.

EDWARD: Don't touch the little fellow.

MICHAEL: I'm not laying a finger on him.

EDWARD: I can't look. What's happening?

MICHAEL: It's all right, we're flying again.

EDWARD: Good man, Chitty-Chitty, good man.

MICHAEL: I think Chitty-Chitty might be a girl.

EDWARD: Where's she heading for now?

MICHAEL: She's flying west, over England, she's passing Birmingham, and Liverpool, you take over. Tell me where we are.

EDWARD: Jesus, I can see it, home, Ireland. Look at it. The shape of it. The colour. Green, it is green. I can see the colour

green again. Good girl, Chitty-Chitty. Keep going. Down,
down, down. Have we landed?
MICHAEL: Yes, safely.
EDWARD: Then drive.
MICHAEL: Where?
EDWARD: Just drive. It's Christmas Day. Drive me to where we
go on Christmas Day. I want to wander through the rows of
graves. I want to see his, my father's grave. I have to talk to
him. That's all. Talk to him.
(*Silence.*)
Da, it's me. It's Edward. Your son, do you remember? Do
you recognize me?
(*Silence.*)
I've been away for a while, Da. Do you know me?
(*Silence.*)
Son, I'm going to die, son.
(*Silence.*)
Da, you'll never die. Never.
(*Silence.*)
Yes, I will die, son.
(*Silence.*)
You'll outlive us all, Da.
(*Silence.*)
Will I go to hell, son?
(*Silence.*)
There's no such place as hell, Da.
(*Silence.*)
Pray for me. Pray for me.
(*Silence.*)
I won't see through this night. Do you hear the way I'm
breathing?
(*Silence.*)
Yes.
(*Silence.*)
Yes, I hear the way you're breathing.
(EDWARD *sings.*)
  Tell me a story,
  Tell me a story,

55

Tell me a story and then I'll go to bed.
(*Silence.* EDWARD *laughs.*)
Do you want anything, Da? Anything at all? Tell me a story,
tell me . . .
(*Silence.*)
The priest comes to see me, son. He's saying Masses. Pray
for me. Will I go to hell?
(*Silence.*)
There is a hell, Da. And I'm in it. I am very scared, Daddy.
Please save me. Please get me out of this place. Carry me in
your arms away from here. If you're in heaven, will you save
me?
MICHAEL: Laugh, Edward.
EDWARD: They've beaten me.
MICHAEL: They really have beaten you.
EDWARD: Save me.
MICHAEL: They can hear you crying. Laugh.
(*Silence.*)
Laugh, you bastard, laugh.
(*Silence.*)
Laugh.
(*Lights fade.*)

SCENE NINE

EDWARD *is free from the chain, dressing himself.* MICHAEL *watches.*
There is silence.

EDWARD: Being an Irishman helped me. I don't know what kind
of deal the government would have done.
MICHAEL: Yes.
(*Silence.*)
EDWARD: I'll go to see your Mother first thing.
MICHAEL: Do that.
EDWARD: I'll tell her you're well.
MICHAEL: Yes, please. Put her mind at rest.
EDWARD: I will.

(Silence.)
MICHAEL: Edward, if she's dead –
EDWARD: She's alive, Michael.
MICHAEL: She is. Please give my best wishes to your wife and
    family and tell them how I look forward to seeing them.
EDWARD: I will. I'll tell them all about you.
MICHAEL: Do.
EDWARD: I'll remember everything.
MICHAEL: I'll miss you.
EDWARD: And I you.
    (Silence.)
    Will you be all right?
MICHAEL: Me, despair? Never. Remember, I support
    Peterborough United.
EDWARD: True enough. They're letting me go because of Adam.
    They need a bit of good publicity, I'd say. He's going to save
    us, he's watching over us –
MICHAEL: You're free, and I'm here.
    (Silence. EDWARD *puts on his tie.)*
EDWARD: I never wear these things normally. Better put on a
    good show. They beat me down, didn't they?
MICHAEL: Yes, they did beat you down.
EDWARD: I don't know what I'll do when I get out.
MICHAEL: Go easy on yourself. Don't drink too much.
EDWARD: I won't. I promise. We should be let go together.
MICHAEL: We're not.
EDWARD: Yes.
MICHAEL: When you cried, you were heard. I wasn't. Maybe I
    didn't cry hard enough. Maybe they think I haven't suffered
    enough. Is that what all this is for? To see us suffer? And to
    what end? What is it for? I don't know. I never will. Do you
    know in all the time I've been in here I have never once
    dreamt that I was locked in? Always in my dreams I'm free.
    A free man. And I would really like my dreams to come true.
    Will you tell them that? Maybe the dreams will change
    without you here. Maybe I won't be able to sleep even.
EDWARD: You will. You have to. You have to keep up your
    strength. You're the strongest man I know. I'm – I'm not. I

57

need you. For what it's worth, I'm watching over you.
MICHAEL: That much I know.
EDWARD: Sleep, dream.
MICHAEL: I will. Move, or they might change their minds.
EDWARD: Right, right.
(*From his jacket pocket* EDWARD *takes out a comb.* EDWARD *goes to* MICHAEL. EDWARD *combs* MICHAEL'*s hair, and gives the comb to* MICHAEL. EDWARD *bows his head.* MICHAEL *combs* EDWARD'*s hair.* MICHAEL *gives* EDWARD *the comb.*)
Right.
MICHAEL: Right.
EDWARD: Good luck.
MICHAEL: Good luck.
(EDWARD *leaves.* MICHAEL *stands still. His body convulses. He regains control. Silence.*)
Oft him anhaga are gebideth. Wyrd bith ful araed.
(*Silence.*)
Whither thou goest, I will go with thee, and whither I go, thou shalt go with me.
(*Silence.*)
Right. Right. Good luck
(*He rattles the chains that bind him.*)
Good luck.